AN UNOFFICIAL ROBLOX BOOK

DIARY OF A ROBLOX PRO

Ari Avatar

FOOTBALL SIMULATOR

SCHOLASTIC

Published in the UK by Scholastic, 2026
Scholastic, Bosworth Avenue, Warwick, CV34 6UQ
Scholastic Ireland, 89E Lagan Road, Dublin Industrial Estate, Glasnevin, Dublin, D11 HP5F

SCHOLASTIC and associated logos are trademarks and/or
registered trademarks of Scholastic Inc.

First published in Australia as *Diary of a Roblox Pro: Soccer Simulator*
by Scholastic Australia, 2024

Text © Scholastic Australia, 2024
Cover and inside illustrations © Scholastic Australia, 2024
Series design by Hannah Janzen
Book design by Paul Hallam

ISBN 978 0702 34565 4

A CIP catalogue record for this book is available from the British Library.

All rights reserved.
This book is sold subject to the condition that it shall not, by way of trade or otherwise, be lent, hired out or otherwise circulated in any form of binding or cover other than that in which it is published. No part of this publication may be reproduced, stored in a retrieval system, or transmitted in any form or by any other means (electronic, mechanical, photocopying, recording or otherwise), or used to train any artificial intelligence technologies without prior written permission of Scholastic Limited. Subject to EU law, Scholastic Limited expressly reserves this work from the text and data-mining exception.

Printed in the UK
Paper made from wood grown in sustainable forests and other controlled sources.

1 3 5 7 9 10 8 6 4 2

Scholastic does not have any control over and does not assume any
responsibility for any third-party websites or other platforms, or their content.

www.scholastic.co.uk

For safety or quality concerns:
UK: www.scholastic.co.uk/productinformation
EU: www.scholastic.ie/productinformation

FRIDAY AFTERNOON

"Come with me, Ari," Zeke **BEGGED**.

He was giving me his best puppy-dog eyes, hands pressed together as if in prayer. He was pleading with me.

"No way," I said, shaking my head. "I'll just make a huge **FOOL** of myself. We both know I can't play."

Zeke was asking me to go to the obby football tryouts with him.

I'm not a pro at obbies like Zeke is. Sure, obbies are fun, but I can hardly make it through a normal obby, let alone having to kick a ball through one!

OBBY FOOTBALL is exactly like it sounds. At it's core, it's just like a normal game of football, except for the fact that the pitch is actually an obby course, with raised platforms, channels of water and lava, and frequent earthquakes designed to knock players over.

Zeke was going to **SMASH** it.

He is an **OBBY PRO**. But even though he really wanted us to be teammates, I knew there was no way I would even make the team.

"Come on, bro," Zeke continued his pleading. "For me?"

I didn't want to let him down. And I supposed it couldn't hurt to just show up. Anyway, the coach, Mr Boulder, would take one look at me and know that I wasn't fit for obby football. At least this way I could tell Zeke that I **TRIED** when I didn't make the team.

"All right, let's go before I change my mind," I sighed.

"**YEAH**!" Zeke yelled, giving me a high five.

I sighed again. This was going to be **EMBARRASSING**.

We walked down the front steps of the school, and left the grounds. It was a short walk to the Blockville Football Club. I was relieved to see the normal football pitch. I would have turned right back around if the obby course was set up!

No way would they let **NEWBIES** get out on a real obby football course just yet.

Since I didn't have any football boots (newbie, remember?!) Zeke lent me the spare pair he kept in his football bag. When he first showed me the shoes, I told him that they probably wouldn't fit because my feet are so small, but he got them out anyway and held them against my feet. Turns out, Zeke and I wear the same size shoe, so unfortunately, I was fresh out of **EXCUSES**.

I strapped myself into the boots and walked over to the rest of the avatars on the pitch. I stayed behind Zeke, trying not to be seen. But, **TRIP** spotted me straight away.

"Here to get **BLOXXED**, newbie?" he said, sneering and laughing.

I rolled my eyes. Typical Trip. He was the most **ANNOYING** avatar in all of Blockville, and now that I knew he would be trying out for the team too, I was even less excited about today's tryouts.

"All right, avatars," Mr Boulder's voice **BOOMED** over the noise. "Listen up!"

We immediately fell **SILENT**. A nervous energy filled the air as we waited for Mr Boulder to deliver his next instruction.

"You will split into two teams — red bibs versus blue bibs. I want you to all show me your **BEST**."

Mr Boulder looked directly at me, as if he already knew my best was not going to cut it. I **GULPED**.

One by one, we all walked over to grab a bib from the box. Zeke and I were at the back of the group, so after Zeke bent down to grab a blue bib, there was only one left. I was just about to close my hand around the final blue bib, when Trip shouldered me to the side and **RIPPED** it out of my hands.

"Better luck next time, **NEWBIE**," he laughed, running off onto the pitch. "Besides, I look better in blue!"

Furious, but with no other choice, I grabbed the final red bib and walked over to join the others on the pitch.

We all lined up in the middle of the pitch. The blue team were starting with the ball. I looked around nervously. Then, the whistle blew.

Zeke immediately **KICKED** the ball over to Trip, who ran towards me with a grin on his face. I tried to move out of his way, but I **PANICKED** and somehow tripped over my own feet. When I stood up, I stuck my leg out to steady myself. But in doing so, I accidentally caught the ball with my foot, successfully tackling Trip in the process. **FLUKE**!

I quickly **PASSED** the ball over to Levi, not wanting to be a target for Trip and the blue team for any longer than I needed to be.

Now free from the ball, I took a moment to look around. The middle of the pitch was definitely not the place to be, as everyone was fighting for the ball. So I moved towards the **GOAL POST**, where it was quieter.

But when I turned back around, I saw Levi, in his red bib, running straight towards me with the ball in his possession. He was skilled, but some defenders were starting to gain on him.

After showing off some **MAD** dribbling skills, he spotted me, right in front of the goal. Zeke was coming in for a tackle, so Levi kicked the ball directly to me!

Bro didn't know how **WRONG** that move was!

As the ball flew through the air, Trip appeared out of nowhere and positioned himself between me and the ball. I swear I could hear him laughing.

The ball whooshed through the air, but Trip couldn't control it, and it bounced off his chest as he pushed into me again. This time I fell backwards, my head **SMACKING** into something on my way down. I crashed into the grass with an "oomph!"

Suddenly, **CHEERS** erupted around me, and someone pulled me up onto my feet and patted me on the back. I could only see stars. Faces swam around me until Zeke came into focus.

"That was an **EPIC** header, Ari!" he shouted, as he ran towards me, a huge grin on his face.

I looked towards the goal. The ball was sitting in the bottom left-hand corner. I looked back at Zeke. He was **BEAMING** at me.

"Bro, you totally **SMASHED** it!" he continued, while both red and blue bibs came over to pat me on the back in congratulations.

Couldn't they tell my goal was just a major **FLUKE**?

Mr Boulder strutted over with his arms crossed. His arms were always crossed.

"**GOOD GOAL**, Ari," he said in a gravelly voice. "Everyone is dismissed. I've seen all I need to today. The announcement will be made on Monday morning."

Zeke and I collected our bags and started our walk home from the football club.

"Ari, you were **AWESOME**!" Zeke said.

"It was a complete fluke!" I said. "I didn't even know I'd scored."

"Well, it looked epic," Zeke said.

Surely Mr Boulder would know my goal was an accident. Wouldn't he?

MONDAY MORNING

"The **LIST** is up!" shouted Zeke. He grabbed my arm and pulled me down the school hallway. Jez followed behind us.

I **GROANED**. It was Monday and the obby football team announcement would be up on the board outside Mr Boulder's office. Surely Mr Boulder saw right through my accidental goal, right? He was supposed to be the **EXPERT**.

Zeke was running so fast that I almost ran out of breath trying to catch up. We reached the sports noticeboard. I couldn't look. This was going to be **ROUGH**.

"I made it!" shouted Zeke. Was there ever any doubt?

"Congrats, bro," I said, turning to head back down the hallway, but Zeke grabbed my shoulder.

"So did you!! We're **TEAMMATES**!"

I stared at Zeke with my mouth open. He had to be joking.

"IRL?" I pushed past him, and there on the page was my name, **ARI**.

"Congrats to *you*, Ari," Zeke said laughing.

"This is **AWESOME**, Ari!" Jez added.

"Um, thanks, guys. But this has to be a mistake."

"No way, not after that **AMAZING** goal," Zeke said, clapping me on the back. "Says here that training starts this afternoon at the Blockville Football Club. We can head there together after school."

The bell rang and Zeke immediately bounced down the corridor to his next class, shouting that he would see us later. I was still in too much **SHOCK** to move. I hardly noticed as Jez put a hand on my shoulder.

"Believe in yourself, Ari," she said encouragingly. "I know this is something you've never done before, but that can be fun. And who knows, you might even surprise yourself." She patted me on the back in support and then walked off to her class.

Ugh. What had I just gotten myself into?

MONDAY AFTERNOON

Zeke and I had planned on walking to the football club together, but Miss Markson wanted to talk to me about my recent maths exam, so Zeke left without me. He was already running laps by the time I arrived at the pitches for training. Late.

GROAN.

The team was made up of all the usual sporty kids, including Trip,

Levi and Elle. Fantastic.
Now Trip would see how bad I really was. I prepared myself for maximum embarrassment.

Mr Boulder **KICKED** a ball in my direction. "Ari, get moving. You're late." Off to a great start.

I grabbed a ball and kicked it gently over to the first drill. There were bright orange cones set up in two lines to make a **ZIG ZAG**. Some of the other kids were already skilfully moving the balls around the cones. Zeke was halfway through the drill and his feet were moving so fast! He made it look easy.

"I want to see you **DRIBBLE** the ball side to side between the cones. Always use your outside foot. It's all about ball control, Ari," Mr Boulder said.

Easy for him to say, I thought.

I had absolutely zero control over a football.

I dribbled the ball towards the first cone. I went to the right, but when I came back to the left, I **TRIPPED** over my own foot.

OOOF.

I hit the ground head-first, seeing stars. And then I heard the laughter.

I slowly lifted my head from the grass to see Trip laughing so hard he was holding his stomach. Zeke looked worried. Thankfully, he wasn't laughing, but the rest of the team had joined in with Trip. Mr Boulder looked at me with the same look my mum gives me when I try getting out of a chore with a lame excuse. At least he wasn't laughing.

"Mr Boulder, how are we supposed to win the big game if Ari can't even kick a ball without ending up on the **GRASS**?" Trip complained. A fresh wave of laughter surrounded me. "That's enough," Mr Boulder said firmly. "Ari get up off the grass and give me five laps of the pitch." Mr Boulder stood looking down at me, his arms crossed. He still wasn't laughing, even though I kinda wished he would — then he wouldn't be so **SCARY**.

I started jogging and as I ran off on my first lap, I could hear Trip behind me, "And Ari, watch your feet. We wouldn't want to damage any more grass." The laughter started all over again. "What a **NEWBIE**."

As I continued to run around the pitch, the laughter followed. I swore I was never coming back.

MONDAY NIGHT

> **Zeke:** You there, bro?

I'd been ignoring Zeke's messages all evening. I felt bad that he was still so excited for me to be joining the team, but I was too **EMBARRASSED** from the disaster at training earlier this afternoon to reply.

I left his message open while I returned to my maths homework. But Zeke wasn't ready to give up.

Zeke: Don't listen to Trip. He's not even that good at obby football.

I typed in a quick reply.

Ari: Well, he's better than I am.

Zeke: You just need to train, then you'll get better.

Ari: Are you kidding? I'm not going back.

Zeke: But we're teammates! You've gotta come back. I'll even help you train.

I sighed. Zeke was a great friend, but he was delusional if he thought a little training would **MAGICALLY** make me good at obby football. But he persisted.

> **Zeke:** I'm not letting you quit. See you at training tomorrow. Ltr.

Great. Now how was I going to get out of it? If I quit, everyone would know I was a loser and, worst of all, Zeke would be disappointed. I knew that training would help, but it wouldn't be fast enough. I needed to be better **NOW**.

TUESDAY MORNING

The next morning I walked through the school gates with my head down, hoping to **HIDE** from anyone who would have seen my fail yesterday.

I knew that I wouldn't be any good at this obby football thing. Zeke was the one with mad skills, not me. But despite yesterday's fail, he still **BELIEVED** in me. I didn't understand it.

Jez met up with me as I reached the steps to the main building.

"Hey, Ari. How's it going?" Jez said casually. A little too casually.

"So, I guess you heard about **TRAINING**, then?"

"Ah, yeah. I'm sorry, Ari."

"All good," I said, kicking a loose rock off the bottom step. "It's not like I'm going back."

Jez looked **SURPRISED**. "But you have to go back! Zeke has been looking forward to playing obby football with you for ages. Besides, Mr Boulder picked you for the team, and he knows what he's doing. You'll just have to train a bit more."

"You weren't there, Jez," I said, feeling hopeless. "My success during tryouts was a **FLUKE**. Then at training, I was eating grass after the first touch of the ball. No thanks." I glared back at her.

"Why don't you ask Zeke if he will help you train? We both know he's **AWESOME** at this stuff."

"I think I'm beyond help—"

THWACK!

A football bounced off my head.

THWACK!

Another ball hit my knee and I buckled, falling to the ground. A familiar laugh sounded from the top of the stairs.

"Oops, sorry, Ari," Trip said sarcastically. "I forgot you were **ALLERGIC** to footballs."

A wave of **LAUGHTER** started as those around us joined in, including Levi and Elle, who were on either side of him with smug smiles on their faces. Jez looked furious.

Trip had a large, black lumpy bag slung over his shoulder. He raised an eyebrow as he stood on the top step and opened the bag. A wave of footballs **BOUNCED** down the stairs, coming straight towards me. A ball hit me on the head as even more people gathered around, laughing and pointing at me on the ground.

"See you at training, **NEWBIE**!" Trip laughed as he walked through the front door and into the school building.

Ugh. So much for hiding. My face **BURNED** red as I turned to Jez and she offered me a hand up.

"Still think I can be helped?" I asked, brushing dirt off my clothes.

Jez looked at me, her head tilted to the side, deep in thought. "You know, I've been studying an experimental **CODE** that can be adapted to the body through hardware. The idea is that the mind would think something, and the coded hardware would allow the body do it," she looked at me **MISCHIEVOUSLY**, her eyes bright with a genius idea. "What if I could code some football boots that would be able to help you play?"

"Is that even possible?" I asked.

"I'm about 99% sure it is," Jez was excited now.

I grinned. I was more than 99% sure that if it *could* be done, then Jez was the person to do it. She's the absolute **QUEEN OF TECH** and her coding abilities have gotten us out of trouble on so many occasions.

"Jez, you are **AMAZING**," I praised, pulling her into a hug. "Incredible even!" I then dug into my bag for Zeke's boots and handed them

over to her. I started to feel
a bit more hopeful.

Maybe this was the answer to all
my problems.

TUESDAY AFTERNOON

DING DING DING.

Finally! I shot off out of my seat and headed straight to the classroom door.

"Sorry, Mr Rockface!" I yelled out. "I have obby football training and I can't be late!"

I ran into the corridor, past the lockers, and **RACED** through the front of the school.

As planned, Jez stood at the top of the stairs holding Zeke's spare boots. Man, she was **QUICK**.

She handed them over with a grin.

"Thanks, Jez. I owe you **BIG TIME**."

"They connect to this," she explained, handing me a small

black ear bud. "It goes in your ear and it will **SYNC** with your thoughts. All you have to do is think about what you need to do on the pitch, and the earpiece will communicate that to the boots."

"You're **AWESOME**, Jez," I said, amazed at her skills. "But I gotta go, before I'm late!"

I hurried down the steps, pushing past everyone else and ran all the way to Blockville Football Club. By the time I arrived at the obby football pitch, I was well and truly out of breath.

"Ari, you're late again," Mr Boulder said. His arms were **CROSSED** against his chest, as usual. I'm not sure his arms could even straighten.

"Yep, but I've already warmed up, Mr Boulder."

He chuckled — like, an actual laugh! "All right then, Ari. Get out there and show me what you've got."

I **GRINNED**, feeling confident that I had more to give than last time.

I quickly switched from my trainers to the coded boots.

I casually lifted my hand to my ear to insert the small black ear bud, trying hard not to draw any attention. It sat **PERFECTLY** and was so small no one would be able to see it.

Ready with my new gear, I ran out onto the pitch. The team had already started a game, with half the players in red bibs, and the other half in blue. Blue looked like they were easily ahead, and no wonder — the team had both Zeke and Trip. I grabbed the final red bib and **JUMPED** into the game.

Someone from the red team let out a groan. "As if we weren't already losing," they complained.

I **LAUGHED**. "Just you wait."

Zeke kicked the ball over to Trip. I ran towards them to get the intercept, but my feet moved so fast that I ended up running straight past the ball.

OOPS.

Okay I thought, *we can work with this.* I doubled back and chased Trip, who was now moving the ball towards the goal. I went in to intercept the ball but **MISSED**. Even though the boots were controlled with my thoughts, it seemed I still needed some practice. On the second tackle, I managed to get the ball off Trip. These boots were **EPIC**!

I turned and kicked the ball past two blue bibs, my feet moving lightning fast. I **DODGED** to the left around another blue player until I was one-on-one with their goalkeeper. I aimed for the top left corner and as my right foot struck the ball, I heard impressed gasps.

The ball flew towards the net like a rocket. **GOAL**!

The goalkeeper looked back at the ball that sat in the net, then over at me in disbelief. His mouth was wide open, completely **SPEECHLESS**. So was I.

Trip stood there, also staring at me. He was **NOT HAPPY** that I'd intercepted the ball.

"Quickest goal ever, Ari!" Zeke shouted with excitement, clapping me on the back.

"**WELL DONE, ARI,**" Mr Boulder said from the sidelines. "It seems someone has been practising."

I didn't say anything. I just smiled back.

"Okay, team, I think it's time we moved on from these easy games and got you all onto the **OBBY** football pitch."

Zeke and I grinned at each other.

Bring it on!

TUESDAY AFTERNOON — A LITTLE BIT LATER

Blockville Football Club had an obby football pitch on the opposite side of the clubhouse. It was where all the big games were held.

I stared up at the obby football pitch, trying to make sense of it. I'd never set foot on one before, and had only seen them on TV. The massive pitch with its complex **OBSTACLES** was a lot to take in! Even Trip looked a little queasy and Levi stood next to him with his mouth hanging open.

"You okay, Ari?" Zeke asked from beside me. "You look worried."

"Yeah, I just realized I have no idea how the 'obby' part of 'obby football' works," I **LAUGHED** nervously, realizing just how dangerous this sport could be.

"Okay, so you still have to score a goal but in obby football, the first goal **WINS**," Zeke explained.

"Well, that seems easy enough," I said.

Zeke laughed. "The goal posts move vertically on a platform, so you can never really take the same shot twice. It also means that the goal could be metres above where you kicked from. But you have to be careful about how close you get — the posts are surrounded by **LAVA PITS**."

He pointed to each part of the pitch as he explained.

"Don't take too long on the centre

pass," Zeke continued, "or flames will **SHOOT** up out of the ground. And as you run down the pitch, big metal poles can break through the ground in front of you and block your path. Or worse."

GULP.

"There's a pit of water on each side of the centre mark that you have to either jump over or swim across. It's as deep as my dad is tall."

Zeke then pointed to the poles along the side of the pitch that looked like they belonged in a car wash, not a football game.

"Those are the batons," he went on. "They **SPIN** during the whole game. If you get thrown up against one of those, you'll end up with bruises from your head to your toes. Throw-ins are **BRUTAL**!"

I nodded as he explained, but my nerves were obvious. "Underneath the grass are electrical lines that can **ZAP** you at any moment and the ground trembles on and off throughout the game. I think that's everything," Zeke ended casually.

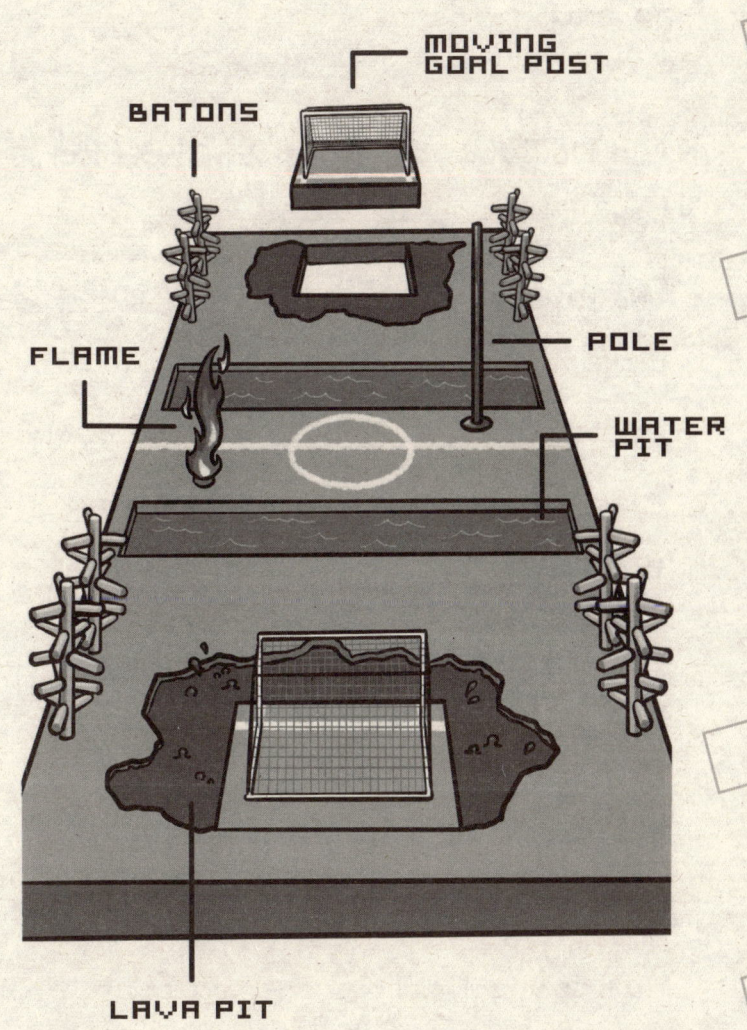

Oh, *that's* it? Easy enough for him to say!

Mr Boulder set us up on the pitch, keeping us in the same teams. He then explained that the rules were the same as normal football, except the pitch was now an obby. Mr Boulder blew the whistle and the game began.

Zeke started with the ball in the centre and immediately passed to Trip. Trip then **KICKED** the ball to another blue player who had leaped across the water that lined the centre mark.

Blue bibs were jumping and swimming across the water to back him up, including Zeke. I thought about jumping across the water and as I reached the edge, my boots took off like they had **SPRINGS** in them.

The ball was passed back to Zeke. By this stage, Trip had made it across the water too.

I ran straight for Zeke, who was aiming his next kick towards Trip, who was positioned up further near the goal. My boots kicked into gear, and I took control of the ball before it could reach Trip. He was even more upset now, having been **INTERCEPTED** twice in this training session.

I moved with the ball down the pitch. I came to the first pool in front of the centre mark and kicked the ball across. My boots were so fast that I was able to jump over the water and land in time to get the ball again.

The ground suddenly **TREMBLED** for the first time and everyone fell down — except for me. I stayed steady on my feet and kept running.

I cleared the second pool of water, regained the ball quickly and headed straight for the goal.
I could see Elle up ahead in her goalie uniform, looking afraid.

Trip finally caught up with me and tried to push me off the ball, but I **DRIBBLED** it like it was taped to my feet. Frustrated, Trip pushed me towards the spinning sideline batons. I kicked the ball with my right foot, towards the centre of the pitch, then I jumped, twisting mid-air until I had completely somersaulted over Trip.

"**WHOA**," said everyone on the pitch at the same time.

Trip continued running towards the batons, and unable to stop in time, got tangled in their spinning trap. But I kept **RUNNING** towards the goal.

Three defenders came at me at the same time. I kicked the ball through the legs of the front defender, and then threw myself on the ground to **SLIDE** through his legs after the ball.

"No way!" shouted one of the

defenders as I jumped to my feet and continued towards the goal. Elle grinned at me from the goal platform, faking confidence. The platform was **MOVING**. It went left, then straight up, then down, then right, then left again.

I pulled my right foot back and let it rip. The ball sailed high into the air, so high that it looked like it was going to go over the goal. But just at the right moment, the goal began to rise. Elle's grin disappeared as she realized that the ball was going to fly right over her head. She tried to jump but couldn't reach it, and the ball flew between her gloves...

GOAL!

"Wooohooo!" shouted Zeke, beaming with pride. He ran over to me, along with the rest of the team. Everyone was patting me on the back and yelling my name. Trip just stared **ANGRILY** as my teammates lifted me into the air.

"Ari! Ari! Ari!" they chanted as they **BOUNCED** me high above them.

"Not bad, Ari," Mr Boulder yelled

from the sideline. As I walked past him, he gave me a high five.

Could this day get **ANY** better?

WEDNESDAY MORNING – REALLY EARLY

After yesterday's epic training session, I figured I should really get some **PRACTICE** in so that I would know how to use the boots properly.

I woke up super early before school, strapped on my coded boots and headed out to the garden, football tucked under my arm. I started **KICKING** the ball against the back wall of the house, practising controlling the ball as it returned.

"Ari, it is way too early for that sort of **NOISE**!" Mum groaned, sticking her head out the back door.

"Sorry, Mum," I said, catching the ball with my left foot. "I just really need to practise for the obby football team."

She looked at me, smiling grudgingly. "Well, despite the noise, I am impressed with your dedication. Don't forget to have breakfast before you leave. You will need fuel for all this sport." She smiled at me again before ducking her head back inside the house.

My stomach **RUMBLED**. She wasn't wrong.

THURSDAY AFTERNOON

"Alright, avatars. Let's discuss Friday night's **BIG GAME** against the Vulcans," Mr Boulder boomed.

We were still **SWEATY** and hot from training.

Mr Boulder crossed his arms tighter, and we all stood up a little straighter. We all knew that was his sign that he meant **BUSINESS**.

"We will meet at the Blockville Football Club right after school for warm up. If you're late, you're out." He looked straight at me. **FAIR**. "The names of our starting team are up on my office door. Check them on the way out. If your name is not on the sheet, it means you are starting on the bench. I still expect you here. Dismissed."

I walked over to Zeke who smiled at me. "**RACE** you to the list?" he challenged, raising an eyebrow.

"You're on," I grinned. Zeke loved to race.

Normally, I wouldn't have stood a chance, but with my **BOOTS** we were even. We raced across the grass, up the stairs, and through the school doors. As we hit the hallway, I pushed ahead a little. I could have sworn I was getting **FASTER**. Maybe the training really was paying off. Or maybe it was just the boots.

I rounded the corner and slid to a stop outside Mr Boulder's office. Zeke caught up seconds later.

"Bro. You are **SUPER FAST**," he huffed.

I laughed and we both turned to the door. There, at the top of the list, was my name with **STRIKER** next to it. Zeke's was just below mine, next to midfield. Trip was down as goalkeeper.

"Congratulations, Ari. You totally deserve it," Zeke beamed.

"Ah, thanks, man." It felt **WEIRD**. I'd never beaten Zeke at anything before. But he was genuinely happy for me.

"Right. I'm off to go practise for the big game! Later!" Zeke walked away down the hallway. I just **STARED** at my name at the top of the list.

"Wait up, Zeke!" I ran after him. "Mind if I join you for some practise?"

"It would be my honour, striker," he grinned.

We made our way back to Zeke's place. His dad had given us some fruit to snack on before training, and after training at Zeke's for half an hour, I was beginning to regret that third orange.

I groaned in pain.

"Not more **SQUATS**," I whined at Zeke.

"Yes, Ari, more squats," Zeke said, ignoring my complaints. "Squats help to strengthen your legs. And stronger legs means you can jump higher and further." No wonder

Zeke was so good at **EVERYTHING**, if this was how he trained.

"I know, I know," I said as my legs shook.

Zeke laughed. "You're going to need **STRONG LEGS** tomorrow. You'll need to cross that water quickly to get the ball moving on our side, striker." He wiggled his eyebrows at me.

I **ROLLED** my eyes. But I knew he was right. Even though I already had the boots, it couldn't hurt for my body to be stronger, too.

FRIDAY AFTERNOON

The sun was shining. The birds were chirping. And the school bell was ringing, signalling the end of the day. **FINALLY**!

I grabbed my bag and ran out of the classroom and into the corridor. I **WEAVED** through the other avatars and a few teachers, ignoring everyone in my path, including Mr Rockface, who was handing out papers to his students.

I sped past them all, too focused on getting to the Blockville Football Club on time. So when my shoulder **KNOCKED** into something hard, I didn't even have time to turn around — I couldn't be late for the big game!

But despite my best efforts to get out of school quickly, I kept getting stopped by avatars wanting to cheer me on and encourage me.

"Go **SMASH** it, Ari!"

"Good luck this afternoon, striker!"

"Woohoo, Ari! Win us the game!"

I **GRINNED**. It felt good.

But it also meant that by the time I arrived at the pitch, I was late. Again.

"Sorry, Mr Boulder," I said, puffing from the run. "I tried. I really did."

But Mr Boulder didn't seem upset. Instead, he grunted and pointed to the pitch where the team was already warming up. "Go join the others. It's a good thing you're our **BEST PLAYER**," he said.

But before I could run onto the pitch, Zeke arrived. *Huh.* He was never late.

"Sorry, Mr Boulder," he huffed. "Mr Rockface **DROPPED** a whole bunch of papers outside his classroom and everyone was just stepping all over them, so I helped him pick them up." Zeke looked at Mr Boulder with a nervous expression.

"Not good enough — you're lucky I don't start you on the bench." Mr Boulder **FROWNED**.
"I want 20 push-ups before you join the others."

Zeke sighed and got down to start his push-ups. My heart sank. I must have **KNOCKED** Mr Rockface over in my rush to get out of school.

As I laced up my boots, I could hear Zeke count each push-up.

"Four ... five ... six..."

I jogged onto the pitch to join the others, feeling **AWFUL**.

After our warm-up, the stands began to fill with people. Avatars from all across Blockville were coming to watch us play against the Vulcans. Soon, every seat was filled, and cheers floated through the air.

I saw Mum, Dad and Ally in the crowd, **WAVING**. They looked proud.

"All right, team," Mr Boulder yelled over the growing noise. "You know how this works — first to score wins. The Vulcans are big competition. They're strong and they're fast. They won the league last year so we can't slack off. This is what we've trained for. Tackle hard, run fast, and if in doubt, get the ball to Ari."

We all high-fived and moved out to our positions on the pitch. The atmosphere was **ELECTRIC**.

Suddenly, I felt a drop of rain. Just a small one. Then it was followed by another. And another. Soon it started sprinkling. And then it was really **RAINING**.

Water pooled on the ground as the rain got heavier.

The referee blew the whistle, signalling the start of the game, and the ball was passed to me. Just then, I noticed sparks coming from my boots. Then they burst into **FLAMES**! Flames as high as my knee! I passed the ball back to Zeke to get it away from me. My feet felt like they were burning inside my boots! I need to get this fire put out — ASAP!

"Take the centre pass faster, Ari," yelled Mr Boulder.

He must have assumed the fire had come from the obby football pitch, because I was too slow with the pass. At least that meant he had no idea about my coded boots — which currently felt like they were **MELTING** off my feet.

I jumped into the water. It soothed my feet and the smoke coming from my boots puffed out. But as I took a step through the water, it felt like I was walking through mud. That was **STRANGE**, since the boots should have made it easier — oh no! The boots no longer worked! The water must have **DESTROYED** the electronics and now the shoes were nothing more than ordinary football boots. I was absolutely no use to the team. What was I going to do?!

I steadied myself. All I could do was try and keep up, and not **EMBARRASS** myself too much. For Zeke. For my teammates.

I waded through the water and back to the centre mark, and as soon as I made it onto the grass, Zeke called out to me.

"Run forward, Ari!" Zeke yelled as he caught the ball at the edge of the pool I just left. He wanted me to jump over the next section of water and take the ball once I was on the other side.

Without thinking, I immediately **LEAPED** across the second pool. It was only once I was in the air and halfway across that

I remembered that the boots were dead. Amazingly, I landed on the other side, and on my feet as well!

"Epic!" Zeke cried out, and then he kicked the ball across the water. It landed at my feet. I took it and ran with it, concentrating hard. Despite that epic jump, I still didn't have the boots to keep me steady, and I really didn't want to **TRIP** over my own feet.

A Vulcan player approached to take the ball from me, but I saw Elle on my left and kicked the ball over to her. Thankfully, it landed in a good place for Elle to take it and run towards the goal. It wasn't a perfect pass, but it wasn't bad either.

Suddenly, the ground started to **SHAKE**. Elle was doing a great job, but she had three players on her. She kicked the ball over to Levi, who continued with the ball to the goal post. But he also became overwhelmed with Vulcan defenders.

"I'm here, bro!" I shouted, and quick as **LIGHTNING**, Levi weaved through his defenders and passed the ball to me. By the time my feet touched the ball, the ground had just stopped shaking.

Another of our teammates was free up ahead. I didn't want the ball longer than I had to, and definitely not long enough to show everyone how bad I was, so I passed. Then I continued towards the **GOAL**. The last defender was there and tried to push me off to the side, towards the spinning batons. I **DUCKED** and threw myself through his legs, landing even closer to the goal.

I was not keen on ending up with a body full of bruises.

Standing just in front of the pit of lava that separated the goal platform from the rest of the pitch, I surveyed the game. Zeke had the ball again and was running straight towards me. Two **DEFENDERS** on either side of him were trying to move him away from the ball.

"Ari!" was all he said as he kicked the ball towards where I stood, right in front of the goal. I raced to meet it, and then looked around.

The goal was moving side to side, at around the middle of its maximum height. It started its descent, so I closed my eyes and **KICKED**.

FRIDAY — SECONDS LATER

"WOOOOOOOO!"

Cheers erupted from the stands. I had scored. We had **WON** the game!

And I did it without the coded boots!

Zeke ran up to me, both hands open for high fives. "That was so awesome," he said. "You nailed it!"

"Nah, you did all the hard work, I just kicked it in."

"**TEAMWORK** makes the dream work," he laughed.

Zeke and I turned and started making our way to the sideline where the rest of the team had already started celebrating. But as we approached the pools near the centre mark, the ground suddenly began to tremble.

A **SCREAM** rang out from the other end of the pitch. Zeke and I whipped our heads around to see who had made the noise.

Trip was still standing on the goal platform, which had frozen in its position at the top of its path, metres above the ground. It was now shaking **VIOLENTLY**, which was not supposed to be happening. The platform started to sink on one side.

The game was over ... why hadn't the pitch stopped shaking?

Suddenly **CRACKS** began to appear all over the obby football pitch — to the left, to the right, and under our feet. The obby was **MALFUNCTIONING** and we were stuck in the middle of it!

The cheers turned to screams as the rest of the players ran off the pitch to the safety of the stands. Some even took on the twirling baton machines to get away from the **TREMBLING** pitch.

Zeke and I looked towards the goal cage that was **TILTING** more and more by the second. Trip was holding on to one side of the goal frame as the other side continued to sink.

"**TRIP**!" Zeke yelled.

The cracks on the pitch got bigger and bigger and Zeke and I quickly found ourselves standing on an island of grass. We were surrounded on one side by the lava from the goal, and on the other side by water from the centre pools that slipped through the cracks. The water collided with the lava in front of us, **HISSED** and steamed up.

It was hot all around us. So hot we were breaking a sweat just standing there.

Trip screamed as the platform sank lower. "**HELP ME**!"

I looked at Zeke. "We can't leave him there. We should help. We're teammates, right?"

"Teammates," he agreed. "If we go now, we should be able to **JUMP** from one island of grass to the next. But we have to go now before the shaking makes the cracks bigger."

He was right. Even as we stood there, the ground continued to shake and the little grass islands got further and further apart.

"**NOW!**" Zeke cried, and we jumped across the crevice to the next piece of grass. We landed on our feet and looked for the next place to jump.

"There," I pointed out another island to Zeke and we jumped again. The ground continued to shake, so we **GRABBED** on to each other's shoulders for balance.

We **JUMPED** again and again, from island to island, while the cracks grew bigger. We slowly made our way towards the goal platform.

Trip was holding on, but barely. As we got closer we could see that his grip was beginning to **SLIP**.

By now, the heat was getting unbearable. We approached the area underneath where the goals were suspended.

"Now what?" I asked Zeke as I wiped my sweaty forehead.

In a moment of perfect timing, a metal pole **EMERGED** from the ground of the island in front of us. Zeke looked at me and grinned.

"**GOING UP?**" he asked, and I laughed, despite being scared.

We jumped over to the next island and gripped the pole.

"If we climb up there, we should be able to get close enough to help Trip," Zeke said.

I nodded in agreement, then we both took off our boots so we could get a better grip with our feet. The ground was warm underfoot.

I started up the pole first. It was difficult because I was all sweaty and my hands kept slipping, so I **CLIMBED** slowly and carefully. I also didn't look down as we climbed. That is never helpful.

Finally, I reached the edge of the goal platform, Zeke right at my feet.

"Now what?" I called behind me.

"I'm going to hold your legs.

That way you can use your arms to help Trip," yelled Zeke.

I shuffled up the pole until I was sitting on the edge of the goal platform. My feet were on Zeke's shoulders, and I held my arms **OUTSTRETCHED** to Trip.

"Trip!"

Trip turned towards my voice and his eyes **WIDENED** as he saw me positioned on the sinking end of the platform.

"It's going to fall, Ari," he said,

sounding panicked. "The whole thing is going to fall!" Trip looked really scared.

"Listen, Trip. You need to let go and slide down the platform towards me. I'll catch you."

"I can't, Ari, I'll fall."

"No, you won't. Just **FOCUS** on me."

Trip looked down at me but stayed exactly where he was, frozen with fear. He wasn't going to move without help.

"I'm going to climb up to Trip," I yelled to Zeke.

"Be **CAREFUL**," he yelled back.

Oh, I planned on it. I gripped the side of the platform and slowly made my way up the incline.

"Trip," I said. "I'm here. You just need to grab my hand and I'll lower you down to Zeke. I promise you'll be okay."

Trip looked at me. "Don't you dare **DROP** me, Ari," he yelled, his voice wavering. Classic Trip.

I shook my head in disbelief, and reached my arm towards him, which he grabbed on to with surprising force. I then **ANCHORED** myself to the goalpost while I lowered him down the platform towards Zeke.

"Almost there," Zeke yelled. "Got him!"

I watched Trip slowly push himself on to the pole.

But before I could slide down the platform to join Trip and Zeke on the pole, the platform **JERKED**. The force of the shaking had cracked the platform right down its centre. The goal platform was now two separate islands that were drifting apart with each second that passed.

Now what was I going to do?!

"Ari!" Zeke yelled. "I'm still here, but you're going to have to jump. The gap is too big."

I started to panic. There was **NO WAY** I was going to make it.

"You can do this, Ari," Zeke shouted from the pole. I could hear in his voice how much he **BELIEVED** in me.

I thought back to the jump I had made over the water during the game earlier. I had leaped over the two-metre pool without the coded football boots. Zeke was right. I could do this. And besides, I kind of had to. I **SWUNG** from where I was hanging on to the edge of the goal, gaining momentum.

One ... two ... three!

On three, I let go of the goals, feet flinging forwards, the top half of my body following quickly. As I flew across the gap I **STRETCHED** my hands out to catch the pole, or, worst-case scenario, for Zeke to catch me. I tried not to think about the actual worst case scenario, which was that I would end up **HURT** on the ground below.

My hands hit the pole and I immediately **WRAPPED** my legs around it.

"Another epic jump, Ari," said Zeke, grinning up at me.

"Inspiring," Trip cut in sarcastically, despite his obvious fear. "Now, how are you going to get me down?"

"We climb down," Zeke said. But Trip was still scared, so Zeke tried reassuring him. "You've got Ari above you and me below, there's no way you could fall.

We've got you."

Trip then gave a very small nod, too **AFRAID** to even move his head.

"That means you can move now, Trip," I said.

"**UGH**, you're so bossy, Ari," he complained, but at least he began to slide down the pole. Very slowly.

"You're very welcome for the rescue, Trip. It was our pleasure." Below us, Zeke **LAUGHED** at my sarcasm.

But Trip only grunted, as if he had just realized that he still depended on us to get down.

We all slid slowly down the pole, careful not to end up piled on top of each other. Slowly, slowly we got closer to the ground.

When we reached the bottom, we were standing on a grass island with Trip. We all puffed, **EXHAUSTED** from the effort.

"Now what?" Trip said frantically.

Zeke and I looked around. The

ground had stopped trembling, but the cracks had gotten so wide that it was clear we weren't going to be able to **JUMP** ourselves to safety.

Then I heard Jez's voice call out. "Over here!"

On the sideline, behind where the goals should have been, stood Jez with a long **PLANK** of wood.

"You guys look like you could use a hand," she grinned.

Could we ever!

Jez lowered the plank over the crack, creating a **BRIDGE** between us and firm ground. She held on to her end so it didn't slide around.

"You'll have to be quick," she said.

"If the ground starts to shake again the gap will get bigger and I'm not sure it will reach you."

Trip immediately **PUSHED** past Zeke and me, hurrying across the plank to safety. Typical.

I walked steadily across the plank to find Jez's hand outstretched to help me at the other end. Zeke was right behind me, and fell onto the grass on the other side, **KNOCKING** me over. We lay there breathing loudly. And then we started to laugh, all of us happy to be safe on the ground.

"We would have been **TOAST** without you, Jez," I said, looking up at our friend.

"Looks like Trip would have been toast without the two of *you*," Jez responded, nodding over to where Trip was.

We then watched as he ran over to his mum. The mayor held him tightly and fussed over him.

"Oh, my baby. You were so **BRAVE**." She wiped his hair and face.

"I sure was," he replied confidently,

leaning in to her smothering.

I guess that meant there was no thanks coming our way.

Jez offered a hand to each of us, pulling us up off the ground.

"Thanks, Jez," I said. "For everything."

She knew exactly what I meant. "You would have worked it out yourself — you're better than you think you are." She **WINKED** at me.

MONDAY MORNING

I walked up the front steps of school slowly. Very slowly. Every muscle in my legs **BURNED** from Friday's obby football match, and my hands felt like big numb blocks from climbing that pole. I definitely wouldn't be giving out high-fives any time soon.

Standing just inside the front door, I could hear Trip **RETELLING** the story of his narrow escape.

"And then I told those two newbies that we had to climb over each other, otherwise we wouldn't be able to slide down the pole."

"TOTAL NEWBIES," chimed in Levi.

"Hey, guys," I said to Zeke and Jez, who were hanging near our lockers.

"You played an **AMAZING** football game on Friday, Ari. I knew you'd win us the game!" Zeke said, looking proud.

But I immediately felt bad. I had

thought a lot over the weekend on what I was about to say next.

"Listen, Zeke, I have a confession," I started, avoiding his gaze. But I knew he deserved the truth. "I was only good at playing because I **CHEATED**."

Zeke looked confused and went to speak, but I continued. "I had coded boots that were designed to make me a great football player. I'm sorry I deceived you. And that I cheated."

I hung my head. I really did feel

terrible. Zeke had been my best friend since we were born, and I hate that I had **LIED** to him.

"You were wearing them the whole time?"

"Yeah. But the **RAIN** at the start of Friday's match made them short circuit or something. The fire at the start was my boots malfunctioning."

Zeke was quiet for a few seconds. "So," he started slowly, "you didn't technically use them during the game? Ari — you did all that

AWESOMENESS all by yourself!"

WAIT, WHAT?!

Zeke was still supportive. He still believed in me. I was just glad I hadn't ruined our friendship over a sport.

"Just don't tell Trip where you got coded boots or else he will want some," Zeke laughed.

"Ummmmm, Zeke?" Jez spoke up quietly from the side. "My turn to confess. The coded boots were my idea. I coded them for Ari. I'm sorry."

My jaw **DROPPED** at her confession. She didn't deserve to take the fall for me. "No, Jez," I cut in. "I'm the one who should be sorry. I shouldn't have dragged you into this."

Zeke looked between us both and then **CRACKED UP** laughing.

"Jez you're a genius! And Ari, you won the game for us, even without the boots! That extra training **DEFINITELY** paid off."

I looked at both my friends with pride. "I think winning the game was the *least* impressive thing we did on Friday."

We all laughed and walked down the hallway, **IGNORING** Trip's third retelling of how he saved the day.

ALSO AVAILABLE: